G000075638

little book of

Champagne
Cocktails

little book of

Champagne
Cocktails

hamlyn

First published in 2001 by Hamlyn,
a division of Octopus Publishing Group Limited
2–4 Heron Quays, London E14 4JP

British Library Cataloguing-in-Publication Data
A catalogue record for this book is available from the British Library

ISBN 0 600 60436 5

Printed in China

Notes for American readers

The measure that has been used in the recipes is based on a bar measure,
which is 25 ml (1 fl oz). If preferred, a different volume can be used
providing the proportions are kept constant within a drink and suitable
adjustments are made to spoon measurements, where they occur.

Standard level spoon measurements are used in all recipes.
1 tablespoon = one 15 ml spoon
1 teaspoon = one 5 ml spoon
Imperial and metric measurements have been given in some of the recipes.
Use one set of measurements only.

UK	US
caster sugar	granulated sugar
cocktail cherries	maraschino cherries
cocktail stick	toothpick
double cream	heavy cream
drinking chocolate	presweetened cocoa powder
icing sugar	confectioners' sugar
jug	pitcher
lemon rind	lemon peel or zest
single cream	light cream
soda water	club soda

SAFETY NOTE The Department of Health advises that eggs should not be
consumed raw. This book contains recipes made with raw eggs. It is prudent
for more vulnerable people such as pregnant and nursing mothers, invalids,
the elderly, babies and young children to avoid these recipes.

Contents

CHAMPAGNE CLASSICS 8
As well as the Classic Champagne Cocktail, there are many other well-known Champagne cocktails, among them Buck's Fizz and Black Velvet. This chapter features all the best-known and best-loved classics.

SUMMER CHAMPAGNE 32
There is nothing nicer and more refreshing than a chilled Champagne cocktail on a summer's day. This chapter features just the thing to take your thirst away – a Summer Cup, Fruit Sparkler or Raspberry Sorbet Fizz perhaps?

CHAMPAGNE SPIRITS 70
Not for the faint-hearted, this chapter includes a heady mix of Champagne combined with gin, brandy, Pernod, whisky and vodka in a selection of mouth-watering cocktails. Try a French '75 or a Paddy's Night, guaranteed to make the party go with a swing.

Introduction

Champagne has launched thousands of ships, toasted millions of weddings and birthdays worldwide, and shared countless untold moments between two people. Champagne is the drink of celebration.

Sparkling wines are now made all over the world, but only wines from the Champagne region of northern France can be graced with the name Champagne. The region lies 90 miles north-east of Paris near the Belgian border, and is characterized by its chalky soil, which provides good drainage for the vines and reflects precious sunlight and heat. The cool climate of the region also helps to develop the distinctive flavour of the wine as the grapes here ripen slowly, allowing them ample time to pick up the important flavouring components.

There are a few simple rules that will enable you to get the most from your precious bottle. Champagne should be served in long-stemmed flutes or tulip-shaped glasses. These are designed to enhance the flow of bubbles and to concentrate the aromas of the wine. Avoid serving Champagne in chilled glasses as you will not be able to appreciate the full flavour. The Champagne coupe, or saucer-shaped glass, was once popular for serving Champagne, but it was not designed with Champagne in mind and is not really suitable for appreciating the drink to its full potential.

Champagne should be served chilled, between 43 and 48°F (about 7°C). At this temperature the aroma and flavour are best appreciated. To chill Champagne to this level, place the unopened bottle in an ice bucket containing half ice and half water for 20–30 minutes. When opening Champagne, keep a finger or thumb over the cork as you remove the foil and the wire cage. Hold the bottle at 45° away from you and from anyone else. Hold the cork and gently turn the bottle in one direction, turning the bottle and not the cork. The cork should not pop, which results in wasted bubbles, but slip out of the bottle with a sigh. Before pouring, wipe the neck of the bottle clean with a linen cloth. Then begin by pouring a little into each glass to be filled. Allow the froth to settle, then top all the glasses up to about two-thirds full. This will prevent any Champagne overflowing. If topping up cocktails with Champagne, take extra care to avoid the glasses overflowing as the presence of the other ingredients in the glass will cause the Champagne to fizz.

Once opened, a bottle of Champagne need not be consumed in one sitting. If there is any left close the bottle with a Champagne stopper and it will remain fizzy in the refrigerator for several days.

Although it would be a sin to drink vintage Champagne in any other way than on its own, Champagne does mix well with other drinks. Try the recipes here using fruit juices, liqueurs and spirits, to create some colourful and exciting cocktails.

Sugar Syrup

This may be used instead of sugar to sweeten cocktails. It can be bought, but is simple to make. Put 4 tablespoons of caster sugar and 4 tablespoons of water in a small pan and stir over a low heat until the sugar has dissolved. Bring to the boil and boil, without stirring, for 1–2 minutes. Sugar syrup can be stored in a in a sterilized bottle in the refrigerator for up to 2 months.

Champagne Classics

Classic Champagne Cocktail

1 sugar lump
1–2 dashes Angostura
    bitters
1 measure brandy
4 measures chilled
    Champagne
orange slice, to decorate

Put the sugar lump into a chilled cocktail or Champagne glass and saturate with the bitters. Add the brandy, then fill the glass with Champagne. Decorate with the orange slice.

Serves 1

Kir Royale

2 teaspoons crème de
 cassis
Champagne

Pour the crème de cassis into
a Champagne flute and top up
with Champagne.

Serves 1

Buck's Fizz

60 ml (2 fl oz) orange
 juice
175 ml (6 fl oz)
 Champagne
orange slices, to
 decorate

**This drink can be made in
party quantities in a large
glass jug. Use 250 ml
(8 fl oz) orange juice to a
bottle of Champagne. Be
sure to allow space for the
Champagne to bubble up.**

Pour the orange juice into
a cocktail glass and add
the Champagne. Decorate with
orange slices.

Serves 1

Bellini

2 measures peach juice
4 measures chilled
    Champagne
1 dash grenadine
    (optional)

to decorate
peach slice
raspberries

Mix all the ingredients in a
large wine glass and serve
decorated with a peach slice and
raspberries on a cocktail stick.

Serves 1

Apricot Bellini

3 fresh apricots
1 dessertspoon lemon
   juice
1 dessertspoon sugar
   syrup (see page 7)
2 measures apricot
   brandy
1 bottle Champagne

Plunge the apricots into boiling
water for a couple of minutes.
Remove the skins and stones and
discard. Put the apricots into a
food processor or blender with
the lemon juice. Process until
smooth and sweeten to taste
with the sugar syrup. Add the
brandy to the purée and divide
between 6 Champagne glasses.
Top up with Champagne.

Serves 6

Blue Champagne

4 dashes blue Curaçao
Champagne

Swirl the Curaçao around the sides of a Champagne flute or wine glass to coat. Pour in the Champagne to fill the glass and serve.

Serves 1

Millennium Cocktail

4–5 ice cubes
1 measure vodka
1 measure fresh
    raspberry juice
1 measure orange juice
4 measures Champagne

Put the ice cubes into a cocktail shaker, add the vodka, raspberry juice and orange juice and shake thoroughly. Strain into a Champagne flute and pour in the chilled Champagne.

Serves 1

Black Velvet

125 ml (4 fl oz) Guinness
125 ml (4 fl oz)
    Champagne

Pour the Guinness into a 300 ml
(½ pint) glass and carefully add
the Champagne.

Serves 1

Champagne Punch

250 g (8 oz) caster sugar
2.5 litres (4 pints)
Champagne
1.2 litres (2 pints)
sparkling mineral
water
2 measures brandy
2 measures maraschino
2 measures orange
Curaçao
ice cubes
fruits, to decorate

Put the ingredients into a large punch bowl containing plenty of ice cubes and stir until the sugar has dissolved. Add fruits to decorate.

Serves 15–20

Emerald Sparkler

1 measure Midori
3 measures Champagne
melon wedge, to
    decorate

Midori is a light, fragrant melon-flavoured liqueur.

Pour the liqueur into a Champagne flute and top up with Champagne. Decorate the glass with a melon wedge.

Serves 1

Pernod Fizz

1 measure Pernod
Champagne
lime slice, to decorate

Put the Pernod into a Champagne flute and swirl it round to coat the sides. Slowly pour in the Champagne to fill the glass, allowing the drink to become cloudy. Decorate with a lime slice.

Serves 1

Peach and Elderflower Champagne

2 ripe peaches
4 tablespoons
    elderflower cordial
1 bottle Champagne
elderflowers, to decorate

Plunge the peaches into boiling water for 1–2 minutes. Refresh under cold water and peel off the skins. Halve, stone and roughly chop the flesh. Put the peaches and elderflower cordial in a food processor and process to a smooth purée. Divide the purée between 6 glasses, top up with Champagne and decorate with the elderflowers.

Serves 6

Champagne
St Moritz

4 ice cubes, cracked
½ measure gin
½ measure apricot brandy
½ measure orange juice
Champagne

Put the ice, gin, apricot brandy and orange juice into a cocktail shaker and shake well. Strain into a glass, top up with Champagne and stir.

Serves 1

Ritz Fizz

1 dash blue Curaçao
1 dash lemon juice
1 dash Amaretto di
Saronno
Champagne
lemon rind spiral, to
decorate

Pour the Curaçao, lemon juice and Amaretto into a glass and top up with Champagne. Stir gently to mix and decorate the glass with a lemon rind spiral.

Serves 1

Tip

Amaretto di Saronno is a liqueur made from almonds and apricots, first made in Saronno, Italy, in the 16th century.

Summer Champagne

La Seine Fizz

Caribbean Champagne

$E=mc^2$

Whippersnapper

Summer Cup

Champagne
Romanov Fizz

Loving Cup

Cardinal Punch

Bombay Punch

Champagne Cobbler

Fruit Sparkler

Bubble Berry

Palm Beach Fizz

Scarlet Sparkler

Haiti Punch

Boatman's Cup

Sparkling Sorbet Punch

Rose Cup

Champagne Cup

Cranberry
Champagne Punch

Champagne Ice

Kir Punch

Mango Bellini

Raspberry Sorbet Fizz

Celebration Cocktail

Carlton

La Seine Fizz

1 measure Cognac
½ measure fraise de bois
½ measure lemon juice
dash orange bitters
2 strawberries, chopped
sugar syrup, to taste
3 measures Champagne
½ measure Grand
    Marnier

to decorate
strawberry wedge
mint sprig

Add the Cognac, fraise de bois, lemon juice, bitters and strawberries to a cocktail shaker with some sugar syrup to taste. Shake and strain into a Champagne glass. Top up with the Champagne and pour the Grand Marnier over the top. Decorate the glass with a strawberry wedge and a mint sprig.

Serves 1

Caribbean Champagne

1 tablespoon light rum
1 tablespoon crème de
    banane
1 dash Angostura bitters
Champagne

to decorate
banana slice
pineapple slice
cocktail cherry

Pour the rum, crème de banane
and bitters into a chilled
Champagne flute. Top up with
Champagne and stir gently.
Decorate with the banana,
pineapple and cherry, all speared
on a cocktail stick.

Serves 1

E=mc²

4–5 crushed ice cubes
2 measures Southern
    Comfort
1 measure lemon juice
½ measure maple syrup
Champagne
lemon rind, to decorate

Put the crushed ice into a cocktail shaker. Pour the Southern Comfort, lemon juice and maple syrup over the ice and shake until a frost forms on the outside of the shaker. Strain into a Champagne flute and top up with Champagne. Decorate with a strip of lemon rind.

Serves 1

Whippersnapper

2 peaches, skinned and chopped

2 small dessert apples, peeled, cored and chopped

2 teaspoons chopped stem ginger

1 bottle pink Champagne

16–20 ice cubes

apple slices, to decorate

Put the peaches, apples, ginger and 2 tablespoons of the Champagne into a food processor and blend briefly. Divide between 4 chilled tumblers, top up with the remaining Champagne and decorate with apple slices.

Serves 4

Summer Cup

1 bottle German Riesling,
  chilled
1 bottle Champagne
4 measures Grand
  Marnier
1 dessert apple, cored
  and sliced
1 orange, sliced
6–10 strawberries,
  halved
ice cubes
750 ml (1¼ pints)
  lemonade
mint sprigs, to decorate

Pour the wine, Champagne and liqueur into a chilled punch bowl and add the fruit. To serve, add lots of ice, top up with lemonade and decorate with mint sprigs.

Serves 12

Champagne Romanov Fizz

8–10 ripe strawberries, hulled
125 ml (4 fl oz) orange juice
2 ice cubes
about 125 ml (4 fl oz) Champagne

to decorate
strawberry slice
mint sprig

Put the strawberries and orange juice into a food processor and blend until smooth. Place 1 ice cube in a tall glass and add the strawberry liquid. Top up with the Champagne. Stir briskly and serve immediately.

Serves 1

Variation

Replace the strawberries with ripe raspberries. Sieve the drink before serving to remove the pips.

Loving Cup

8 sugar cubes
2 lemons
½ bottle medium or
    sweet sherry
¼ bottle brandy
1 bottle Champagne

**This is an ideal drink
to welcome guests
on Christmas Day.**

Rub the sugar cubes over the
lemons to absorb the zest. Thinly
peel the lemons and remove as
much of the pith as possible.
Thinly slice the lemons and set
aside. Put the lemon rind, sherry,
brandy and sugar cubes into a
jug and stir until the sugar has
dissolved. Cover and chill in the
refrigerator for about 30 minutes.
To serve, add the Champagne to
the cup and float the lemon slices
on top.

Serves 12

Cardinal Punch

500 g (1 lb) caster sugar
2.5 litres (4 pints)
    sparkling mineral
    water
ice cubes
2.5 litres (4 pints) claret
600 ml (1 pint) brandy
600 ml (1 pint) rum
600 ml (1 pint)
    Champagne
2 measures sweet
    vermouth

Dissolve the sugar in the mineral water, then pour into a large punch bowl containing plenty of ice. Add the remaining ingredients and stir gently. Keep the punch bowl packed with ice.

Serves 25–30

Bombay Punch

1.2 litres (2 pints) brandy
1.2 litres (2 pints) sherry
150 ml (¼ pint)
  Maraschino
150 ml (¼ pint) orange
  Curaçao
5 litres (8 pints)
  Champagne
2.5 litres (4 pints)
  sparkling mineral
  water
ice cubes
fruits and mint sprigs, to
  decorate

Pour the ingredients into a large
punch bowl containing plenty
of ice cubes and stir gently.
Decorate with fruits in season
and mint. Keep the punch bowl
packed with ice.

Serves 25–30

Champagne
Cobbler

I tablespoon icing sugar
1 piece of lemon rind
1 piece of orange rind
shaved ice
Champagne
orange slices, to
    decorate

Place the sugar and lemon and orange rinds in a glass, then fill it one-third full with shaved ice. Top up with Champagne, stir gently and decorate with orange slices.

Serves 1

Fruit Sparkler

1 bottle Riesling, chilled
125 ml (4 fl oz) brandy
1 bottle Champagne
250 g (8 oz) hulled
    raspberries or
    strawberries or sliced
    peaches

Pour the Riesling into a large
punch bowl. Stir in the brandy,
then add the Champagne. Add
the fruit and serve.

Serves 18–20

Bubble Berry

2 raspberries
2 blackberries
½ measure framboise
½ measure crème de
    mûre
3 measures Champagne
blackberry, to decorate

Crush the raspberries and blackberries in the bottom of a Champagne glass. Add the framboise and the crème de mûre. Top up with the Champagne. Decorate the glass with a blackberry and serve immediately.

Serves 1

Palm Beach Fizz

1 measure apricot brandy
1 measure orange juice
¼ measure Grand
   Marnier
Champagne

Put the apricot brandy, orange juice and Grand Marnier into a Champagne flute and stir well. Carefully top up the glass with Champagne.

Serves 1

Variation

Replace the apricot brandy with cherry brandy.

Scarlet Sparkler

1 measure cranberry
    juice
1 measure Cointreau
Champagne
cranberries, to decorate

Pour the cranberry juice and
Cointreau into a tall glass and stir
gently. Top up with Champagne
and pop a few cranberries into
the drink to decorate.

Serves 1

Haiti Punch

2 pineapples, peeled and
    cubed
3 lemons, sliced
3 oranges, sliced
300 ml (½ pint) brandy
300 ml (½ pint) Orange
    Nassau liqueur
2 bottles Champagne

to decorate
pineapple leaf
orange rind spiral

Put the fruit into a large bowl
or jug and pour the brandy and
liqueur over the top. Cover and
chill for several hours. To serve,
pour about 1 measure of
the brandy mixture into a
Champagne flute, top up with
Champagne and some of the
fruit. Decorate each glass with a
pineapple leaf and an orange
rind spiral.

Serves 20

Boatman's Cup

500 ml (17 fl oz) still dry
cider
75 ml (3 fl oz) brandy
600 ml (1 pint) orange
juice
750 ml (1¼ pints)
lemonade
1 bottle Champagne

to decorate
black cherries, halved
1 orange, sliced
melon balls or cubes
mint sprigs

Mix together the cider, brandy
and orange juice. Cover and chill
for 2 hours. Just before serving,
add the lemonade, Champagne,
fruit and mint.

Serves 14–15

Sparkling Sorbet Punch

500 ml (17 fl oz) lemon
sorbet
½ bottle sweet white
wine
1 bottle Champagne
lemon slices, to decorate

Scoop the sorbet into a
punch bowl. Pour in the wine
and Champagne. Decorate with
the lemon slices and serve
immediately.

Serves 10

57

Rose Cup

ice cubes
1 bottle sweet white
    wine
1 bottle pink Champagne
4 tablespoons Southern
    Comfort
450 ml (¾ pint) tonic
    water
4 tablespoons canned
    mandarin segments

Put the ice in a large punch
bowl and pour in the wine,
Champagne, Southern Comfort
and tonic water. Add the
mandarin segments, with
their syrup to taste. Serve as
soon as possible.

Serves 12–14

Tip

For a special occasion,
float rose or marigold
petals on top of the drink.

Champagne Cup

3 ripe peaches, skinned
and sliced
1 orange, sliced
cocktail cherries
3 teaspoons sugar
4 measures Grand
Marnier
4 measures kirsch
1 bottle Champagne

Put the peaches, orange slices,
cherries and sugar into a punch
bowl. Pour in the Grand Marnier
and kirsch and stir thoroughly.
Cover the bowl and chill in the
refrigerator for 1 hour. Pour in
the Champagne just before
serving.

Serves 8–10

Cranberry Champagne Punch

1 litre (1¾ pints)
    cranberry juice
250 ml (8 fl oz) brandy
lime wedges
caster sugar
soda water
1 bottle Champagne

Combine the cranberry juice, brandy and lime wedges in a punch bowl, stir well and add sugar to taste. Add the soda water and Champagne just before serving.

Serves 10

Champagne Ice

250 g (8 oz) sugar
300 ml (½ pint) water
300 ml (½ pint)
    Champagne
juice of 1 lemon and
    1 orange
strawberries, to serve

This is a soft Champagne sorbet, which is perfectly complemented by fresh strawberries. Serve it with spoons.

Put the sugar and water into a heavy saucepan and heat gently until the sugar has dissolved. Stir the Champagne and fruit juices into the sugar syrup, then freeze until slushy. Serve in glasses with the strawberries.

Serves 6

Kir Punch

250 g (8 oz) ripe
    strawberries
3–6 measures crème de
    cassis
3 bottles Champagne
soda water

Place the strawberries in a punch
bowl, add the crème de cassis,
cover and chill for 2 hours. Add
the Champagne and stir, then top
up with soda water to taste.
Serve immediately.

Serves 20

Mango Bellini

3 measures mango juice
pink Champagne

Pour the mango juice into a
Champagne flute and top up
with Champagne. Stir gently
to mix and serve immediately.

Serves 1

Variation

To make a Guava Bellini,
replace the mango juice
with guava juice.

Raspberry Sorbet Fizz

1 scoop raspberry sorbet
pink Champagne
raspberries, to decorate

Place a neat scoop of sorbet in the bottom of a glass. Top up with Champagne, decorate with fresh raspberries and serve immediately.

Serves 1

Variation

Any flavour of sorbet can be used to make a Sorbet Fizz. Peach, apricot and mango are all good choices. Match the fruit decoration to the sorbet.

Celebration Cocktail

1 lemon wedge
caster sugar
3 ice cubes
1 measure brandy
1 dash Bénédictine
1 dash crème de mûre
Champagne

Frost the rim of a Champagne
flute with the lemon wedge and
sugar. Put the ice into a cocktail
shaker and add the brandy,
Bénédictine and crème de mûre.
Shake well, strain into the flute
and top up with Champagne.

Serves 1

Carlton

3 measure orange juice
1 measure Grand
    Marnier
1 egg white
dash of bitters
Champagne
ice cubes

Put the ice into a cocktail shaker
and add the orange juice, Grand
Marnier, egg white and bitters.
Shake well and strain into a glass
and top up with Champagne.

Serves 1

Champagne Spirits

French '75
Bellini-tini
Cheshire Cat
New Orleans Dandy
Paddy's Night
Happy Youth
Gorgeous Grace
Valencia Smile
Royal Flush
Champagne Julep
American Flyer
Champagne Cooler
Eve
Champagne Bayou
Kir Champagne
Head-over-heels

French '75

6–8 ice cubes, cracked
1 measure gin
juice of ½ lemon
1 teaspoon caster sugar
Champagne
orange slice, to decorate

Half-fill a tall glass with cracked ice. Add the gin, lemon juice and sugar and stir well. Top up with chilled Champagne and decorate with an orange slice.

Serves 1

Tip

To make cracked ice, put some ice cubes into a strong polythene bag and hit the bag with a rolling pin.

Bellini-tini

2 measures vodka
½ measure peach
   schnapps
2 teaspoons peach juice
Champagne
peach slices, to decorate

Pour the vodka, peach schnapps and peach juice into a cocktail shaker and shake thoroughly. Pour into a cocktail glass and top up with Champagne. Decorate with the peach slices.

Serves 1

Tip

Use a juicer to make fresh peach juice or, for small quantities, a citrus squeezer could be used.

Cheshire Cat

4–5 ice cubes
1 measure brandy
1 measure sweet
    vermouth
1 measure orange juice
Champagne
1 piece of orange rind
orange rind spiral, to
    decorate

Put the ice cubes into a mixing glass. Pour the brandy, sweet vermouth and orange juice over the ice and stir to mix. Strain into a Champagne flute and top up with Champagne. Squeeze the zest from the piece of orange rind over the drink and decorate with an orange rind spiral.

Serves 1

Tip

To make an orange rind spiral, use a canelle knife to remove a long, thin strip of rind, which should curl naturally.

New Orleans Dandy

4–5 ice cubes
1 measure white rum
½ measure peach brandy
1 dash orange juice
1 dash lime juice
Champagne

Put the ice cubes into a cocktail shaker. Pour the rum, peach brandy, orange juice and lime juice over the ice and shake until a frost forms on the outside of the shaker. Strain into a Champagne flute or tall glass and top up with Champagne.

Serves 1

Paddy's Night

champagne spirits

3 ice cubes, cracked
1 measure green crème
 de menthe
1 measure Irish whiskey
Champagne

Put the ice, crème de menthe and whiskey into a cocktail shaker and shake well. Strain into a large wine glass and top up with Champagne.

Serves 1

Happy Youth

1 measure cherry brandy
juice of 1 orange
1 sugar lump
ice cubes
Champagne

Put the cherry brandy, orange juice and sugar into a glass with some ice. Top up with Champagne.

Serves 1

Gorgeous Grace

1 measure brandy
½ measure Cointreau
4 ice cubes, cracked
Champagne
orange slice, to decorate

Stir together the brandy, Cointreau and ice in a mixing glass. Pour into a Champagne flute and top up with Champagne. Decorate with the orange slice.

Serves 1

Tip

Cointreau is a colourless liqueur flavoured with oranges.

Valencia Smile

2 measures apricot
   brandy
1 measure orange juice
4 dashes orange bitters
ice cubes
Champagne

Pour the apricot brandy, orange juice and orange bitters into a tumbler over ice. Top up with Champagne.

Serves 1

Royal Flush

4 ice cubes, cracked
1 measure brandy
2 measures Cointreau
2 measures grapefruit
    juice
1 teaspoon grenadine
Champagne

Put the ice, brandy, Cointreau, grapefruit juice and grenadine into a cocktail shaker and shake well. Strain into a tumbler or highball glass and top up with Champagne to taste.

Serves 1

Tip
Grenadine is a fruit syrup made from pomegranates.

Champagne Julep

2 mint sprigs
1 tablespoon sugar syrup
    (see page 7)
crushed ice
1 measure brandy
Champagne

Crush the mint with the sugar syrup on the bottom of a glass. Fill the glass with crushed ice, then add the brandy. Top up with Champagne and stir gently.

Serves 1

American Flyer

4 ice cubes, cracked
1 measure white rum
1½ teaspoons lime juice
sugar, to taste
Champagne

Put all the ingredients, except the Champagne, into a cocktail shaker and shake well. Strain into a glass and top up with Champagne.

Serves 1

Champagne Cooler

1 measure brandy
1 measure Cointreau
crushed ice
Champagne
mint sprigs, to decorate

Pour the brandy and the Cointreau into a Champagne glass over crushed ice. Fill the glass with Champagne and stir. Decorate with mint sprigs.

Serves 1

Eve

Pernod
1 tablespoon brandy
1 teaspoon caster sugar
2 teaspoons orange
    Curaçao
pink Champagne

Pour a few drops of Pernod into a
Champagne flute to coat the
sides. Pour in the brandy. Soak
the sugar with the Curaçao until
it has dissolved and add to the
brandy, stirring gently. Top up
the glass with Champagne.

Serves 1

Tip

Curaçao is a sweet,
orange flavoured liqueur
which can be blue, white
or orange. It comes from
the island of Curaçao in
the West Indies.

Champagne Bayou

3 ice cubes, cracked
1½ measures gin
2 teaspoons sugar syrup
    (see page 7)
1 teaspoon lemon juice
Champagne
lemon slice, to decorate

Put the ice into a cocktail shaker
with the gin, syrup and juice.
Shake well and strain into a
glass. Top up the glass with
Champagne and float a lemon
slice on the top.

Serves 1

Kir Champagne

2 measures vodka
3 measures crème de
    cassis
1 bottle Champagne

Put a teaspoon of vodka and
2 teaspoons of crème de cassis
into each of 6 glasses. Top up the
glasses with Champagne.

Serves 6

Head-over-heels

4–5 ice cubes
juice of 1 lime
3 measures vodka
sugar lump
3 drops Angostura bitters
Champagne

Put the ice cubes into a cocktail shaker. Pour the lime juice and vodka over the ice and shake until a frost forms on the outside of the shaker. Put a sugar lump at the bottom of a glass and shake the bitters over it. Strain the contents of the shaker into the glass, top up with Champagne and serve.

Serves 1

Tip

If you roll the whole lime around quite hard on a board with your hand, prior to juicing, you will find you get more juice from it.

INDEX

NEW PHOTOGRAPHY
by William Reavell
Cocktails styled by Andrew
Fitz-Maurice at High Holborn,
95–96 High Holborn, London
WC1V 6LF

**ACKNOWLEDGEMENTS IN
SOURCE ORDER**

**Octopus Publishing Group
Limited**/ Jean Cazals 3, 36,
57, 86 / Neil Mersh 11, 17,
19, 27, 75 / Peter Myers 6–7
background, 41 / William
Reavell front cover, back
cover, 2, 5, 8, 13, 21, 22,
25, 31, 32, 35, 39, 43, 47,
49, 51, 55, 59, 61, 64, 67,
70, 73, 79, 83, 85, 89, 91,
93, 95 / Ian Wallace 45, 68